DRAW *Near*

"The entire liturgical calendar revolves around the two fundamental mysteries of our faith: the Incarnation and the Paschal Mystery. Each year we prepare anew to immerse ourselves in these mysteries by prayerfully keeping the seasons of Advent and Lent. Ave devotionals are sure and steady guides for anyone wishing to grow in holiness and embrace the full spirit of these blessed seasons of the Church."

Fr. Blake Britton
Author of *Reclaiming Vatican II*

"By starting with a verse from the Liturgy of Hours or the Bible, these devotions offer a beautiful compass for navigating the Church's holiest seasons. The format draws us into the daily prayer of the Church and plants us firmly within its universal community."

Allison Gingras
Author of *Encountering Signs of Faith*

"These new Ave devotionals will help Catholics looking for a deeper connection with Christ as they prepare for the Church's great feasts. Written by a former editor of FaithND's daily reflections, they carry the same call to grounded faithfulness that characterizes not only Ave Maria Press, but also the Congregation of Holy Cross and the Notre Dame family of faith."

Dolly Duffy
Executive Director
Notre Dame Alumni Association

DRAW *Near*

DAILY PRAYERS
FOR *Advent* AND *Christmas* 2023

WRITTEN BY JOSH NOEM

AVE MARIA PRESS AVE Notre Dame, Indiana

Nihil Obstat: Reverend Monsignor Michael Heintz, PhD
 Censor Librorum

Imprimatur: Most Reverend Kevin C. Rhoades
 Bishop of Fort Wayne–South Bend
 Given at Fort Wayne, Indiana, on April 26, 2023

Writer
Josh Noem

Founded in 1865, Ave Maria Press is a ministry of the United States Province of Holy Cross.

www.avemariapress.com

Paperback: ISBN-13 978-1-64680-261-6

E-book: ISBN-13 978-1-64680-262-3

Cover image © LinaraArtPrints, www.etsy.com/shop/LinaraArtPrints.

Cover and text design by Katherine Robinson.

Printed and bound in the United States of America.

Welcome to Ave Devotionals

Thousands of Catholics are holding this booklet in their hands, just as you are. Is it too strange to think that these words can connect us all in a meaningful way? As Catholics, we have a name for this kind of thing: *sacramental imagination*. It allows us to see how the visible can make the invisible real—how the prayer booklet in your hands can be a line of connection to a communion of people who live around the world, even some who lived in years gone by. Thank you for joining hands with us as we pray through this holy season of preparation and rejoicing.

Ave Maria Press is one of the oldest continually operating Catholic publishing houses in the country. We were founded more than 150 years ago as a ministry of the Congregation of Holy Cross to honor Mary, support the spiritual needs of our everyday living, and showcase the best American Catholic writing.

Great writing has always been the backbone of Ave Maria Press, and we're proud to have shared the voices of American Catholic giants such as Dorothy Day and Henri Nouwen and Thomas Merton. And our publications support Catholics in every stage of life, whether it's a resource that helps a young couple prepare for marriage, a Bible that helps a new mother find hope in God's faithfulness, a textbook that catechizes a high schooler, or a book that changes the way you walk through the seasons of the Church year.

Though not everything we publish speaks of her explicitly, our work also honors Mary—like her, we are here to fulfill a call to bear God's Word to the world and to help you do the same. At the heart of every Ave book, you can find a small annunciation, an invitation to let God break into our lives in a new way. The words our authors share reflect their yes to this good news; they write to encourage you to say yes, too.

If that feels like a big ask, you're in good company. This is a question we have to answer anew every day, especially during Advent and Lent.

We created these Ave Devotionals to offer daily spiritual touch points through these special seasons. With hands joined in prayer, let us lift up our hearts!

How to Use This Booklet

Your light will come, Jerusalem;
the Lord will dawn on you in radiant beauty.
You will see his glory within you.

This line from the Church's Morning Prayer bookends our Advent journey—we pray it several times, including during the first week of Advent and again on December 23. Through the ages, the Church has held on to the promises carried by this prayer: "Your light will come . . . the Lord will dawn on you in radiant beauty . . . you will see his glory."

Though our search for purpose and meaning winds through darkness, light will come. Though we would rather keep the ugly parts of our lives hidden, radiant beauty will dawn upon us. Though so much of our experience feels ordinary, worn out, and stuck in the mud, we will see his glory within us.

Through faith, we hold to these promises that are fulfilled in the person of Jesus Christ, who was sent into the world to illuminate our lives with beauty and glory. *But what does that mean, really?* The work of Advent is not to somehow summon this beauty and glory ourselves but to simply create room in our hearts for Jesus, who is *already there*, bringing us warmth and light, even in this moment as you read this booklet. The goal of a daily prayer practice during this season is to gently blow on the glowing embers of his presence until they start to flame.

The devotions in this booklet build week to week on themes that have emerged from the Church's many journeys through Advent. The first week is about waking up, the second challenges us to prepare a way for Christ in our lives, the third is focused on rejoicing, and the fourth urges us to receive God's light. The prayers of the Christmas season in the fifth week help us to wonder at the self-gift of God, which we celebrate in the Incarnation.

Each day's entry in this booklet takes a line from the Liturgy of the Hours or a brief scripture passage and uses it as a diving board. Dive in with the brief reflection and two short prayers—one for morning, one for night. We've also offered a traveling question you can carry throughout the day. You don't have to be praying the Liturgy of the Hours (or even be familiar with it) to use this booklet. All you need to know is that these lines come from the Church's prayer through the ages and are well-worn pathways to God.

These simple devotions can shape your prayer with just a few minutes each day. When you can, linger with the phrases and images we've brought forth from the prayers of this season. We kept everything short because the best thing we can do for our prayerful preparation is to create stillness, a holy place where Christ can be born anew in our hearts.

Come, Lord Jesus, come be our light!

⁎

December 3

FIRST SUNDAY OF ADVENT

It is the hour now for you to awake from sleep.
For our salvation is nearer now than when we first believed.

ROMANS 13:11

Sister José Hobday was as close to a John the Baptist figure as we may ever get. Picture in your mind a Franciscan nun and Seneca elder, and you'll have a perfect image of what she looked like. She traversed the desert of the American Southwest in sandals and a dusty Jeep to visit and comfort people living on reservations. She died in 2009 and is well remembered for her talks on spirituality and simple living.

She'd begin a presentation by putting both hands in the air and yelling loudly: *Wake up!* This was before she even picked up the microphone. No introduction, no context. Then she'd repeat it, longer and louder: *Wake up!*

And then she'd step forward, nearly into the front row—her brown, wrinkled hands outstretched like the limbs of an oak sprouting buds in April—and as loudly as she could: *Wake up!*

Whatever else she said about our search for God, it started here: we're asleep and we need to wake up. Our days fall into a rhythm, and if we're not watchful, we get rocked into complacency by the routines of work and home life. Advent echoes Sister José's message: it's time to wake up!

What parts of your life are mired in complacency? God is ready to do something new in you—it is time to get moving; the day is already at hand.

Prayer for Morning

Awaken my soul, O God, and help me remember that you are looking for me even as I search for you this day. In fact, you've already found me. You've been here all along. Even my desire to find you comes from you. Awaken my senses to see and recognize you today, for you are closer to me than I can fathom.

God of love, I begin this day searching for you.

Traveling Question

What part of today feels as if I'm just going through the motions?

Prayer for Evening

Lord, I come to you this evening, remembering that you carried me through the day. Bring me safely through the night, and in the morning awaken in me trust that you will carry me once again. As this week unfolds, let me cling to your closeness.

God of love, I close this day with gratitude, knowing you are searching for me.

December 4

MONDAY OF THE FIRST WEEK OF ADVENT

The voice of the LORD strikes with fiery flame;
and strips the forests bare. The God of glory thunders.

PSALM 29

To see what the psalmist was describing, just think back to footage you've seen of the wreckage left by a hurricane or tornado. If God's voice has the power to rearrange the landscape, it can rearrange our lives as well.

Advent is a time to scramble *inside* that blast radius—to put ourselves in the way of God's Word so it can shake us up. The only way to stay safe is to press into God's transforming love—everything else will be stripped bare.

Prayer for Morning

Almighty God, you love me too much to let me sit comfortably in my old ways. Help me to wake up to the sound of your voice speaking in my life and to start moving with urgency toward you. My very life depends on you.

God of glory, let your power move me today.

Traveling Question

What part of my life needs to be shaken up?

Prayer for Evening

Mighty Lord, you want to transform the geography of my interior life, to clear away what is overgrown and breathe new life into me. Help me to let go of what is weighing me down so that I can respond to you more quickly.

God of glory, you are my strength.

✦

December 5

TUESDAY OF THE FIRST WEEK OF ADVENT

Light that never fades, dispel the mists about us
—awaken our faith from sleep.

We try to make our lives comfortable with routine. We try to wake up at the same time every morning, we have our normal lunch options, and we settle in for a familiar end to the day. But faith connects us to the mystery of God, who is always beyond us, and so it is always nudging us to newness. A faith that is comfortable is dormant.

Prayer for Morning

Creator of heaven and earth, burn away whatever dims the light of your presence in my life, whatever has lulled to sleep my mind and my heart. Help me to see you with clarity, and to feel the warmth of your love.

God of new life, help me turn toward your light today.

Traveling Question

What part of my practice of faith feels comfortable and lackluster?

Prayer for Evening

Creator of heaven and earth, as winter settles in, each day loses more of its grip on the daylight; night falls sooner, and we spend more of our evenings in darkness. Let the waning daylight of this season remind me to cling to your light, which never fades.

God of new life, thank you for sustaining my growth today.

December 6

WEDNESDAY OF THE FIRST WEEK OF ADVENT

You are nearer to us than we to ourselves
—strengthen our faith and our hope of salvation.

With the coming of his Son, Jesus, God proves to us that he is definitively invested in our everyday experience. Nothing is too ordinary or boring or insignificant for God to be involved in—he doesn't have better things to do. Advent is a time to wake up to the reality that God is already closer to us than we can imagine.

Prayer for Morning

God, you are not somewhere above or outside of me, seeking a way in. Help me discover that you are already here, acting in my life through whatever experiences bring me to greater faith, hope, and love.

God of love, be with me in every moment of this day.

Traveling Question

How does God show his presence to me in the small, ordinary experiences of my day?

Prayer for Evening

Because you are Love, God, I did not do anything today that made me more or less worthy of your presence with me. Help me remember that my efforts this Advent are about increasing my capacity to perceive how close you already are to me.

God of love, thank you for being with me in every moment of this day.

December 7

THURSDAY OF THE FIRST WEEK OF ADVENT

Arise, arise! Wake from your slumber, Jerusalem,
shake the chain from your neck,
captive daughter of Zion.

Because this language comes from the Church's prayer, it's easy to read it in a muffled, pacified way. Instead, imagine a drill sergeant turning your bunk over and shouting these words. That's the kind of urgency at play here. It's time to let go of what is holding us back, to rise up and begin anew. Now.

Prayer for Morning

You free me from the prison of my own selfishness, God. Your truth calls me out of the stories I tell myself about who I am and frees me to grow in ways beyond what I can imagine. Help me see how I could be more generous, loving, and faithful.

God of freedom, help me step forward in a new direction of integrity today.

Traveling Question

Which habits act like a chain around my neck?

Prayer for Evening

God, as another night draws near, I am aware of how quickly the day passed. The time to act, the opportunity to change my life, is limited. I don't have forever. Please help me to see clearly what is holding me back from being the person you created me to be. Make me impatient for you.

God of freedom, sharpen my resolve to respond more promptly to you.

December 8

FRIDAY OF THE FIRST WEEK OF ADVENT

SOLEMNITY OF THE IMMACULATE CONCEPTION OF THE BLESSED VIRGIN MARY

I rejoice heartily in the Lord, my being exults in my God

ISAIAH 61:10

This may not be an easy feast day to connect with. Just for contrast, consider the drama of the Transfiguration—we can just picture an otherworldly scene at the top of a mountain with heavenly visitors. Epiphany has a good story with the wise men and the gifts. The embrace between Mary and Elizabeth we hear about on the Feast of the Visitation feels familiar. But the Immaculate Conception—the celebration of the start of Mary's life in the womb of her mother, Ann—can be hard to get a handle on.

Here's the good news we are celebrating with this feast day: from the very start of her life, God equipped Mary for the role she plays for us. And God does the same for us—God gives us what we need to perceive and respond to him.

The support of this kind of grace gives us something to lean on in our Advent journey. We can trust that God not only is calling us to something more but also will provide the means for us to get there.

Put another way: from the very start of your life, God has been working to give you the capacity to encounter him in prayer in this moment today—right now.

As Mary knew, that encounter brings joy. She would have heard and understood what Isaiah meant when he wrote, "In my God is the joy of my soul."

Prayer for Morning

You created me for communion with you, God, and have been working to bring me closer to you since the start of my life. My very desire to know you comes from you. Help me to discover you even within my longing for you.

God of grace, draw me closer to you today.

Traveling Question

How can I support the work God is doing in the lives of other people I meet today?

Prayer for Evening

Mary, our mother, to "rejoice heartily in the Lord" was a way of life for you. You recognized God's presence with you in every moment, even when you encountered challenges and pain. Help me to perceive God at work in my experience.

Mother of grace, pray for me, that I may also trust in God's ever-present love.

December 9

SATURDAY OF THE FIRST WEEK OF ADVENT

The day of the Lord will come like a thief,
and then the heavens will pass away with a mighty roar
and the elements will be dissolved by fire, and the earth and
everything done on it will be found out.

2 PETER 3:10

Advent reminds us that the Lord came to us in the person of Jesus more than two thousand years ago; the Lord comes to us in the here and now of our lives, and the Lord will come to us at the end of time. Each of those comings is disruptive, and the final coming will be definitively so. When that final day comes, it will be too late to begin preparing for it. This is a wake-up call to put our houses in order—to be vigilant.

Prayer for Morning

Lord, everything I know will be changed when your power over my life is fully revealed. Help me bring wisdom and urgency to my day, so that I can welcome you with joy, not fear.

God of truth, destroy anything in my life that resists you today.

Traveling Question

How can I become more watchful for the Lord today?

Prayer for Evening

As the deepest layer of who we are, God, you will still be standing when everything else in my life is gone. Even the things I cannot imagine living without will pass away. But your truth and love for me will remain. Make my faith firm.

God of truth, you made the heavens and the earth—help me grow more confident in the love with which you created me, too.

December 10

Second Sunday of Advent

A voice proclaims:
In the wilderness, prepare the way of the Lord!
Make straight in the wasteland a highway for our God!

Isaiah 40:3

In their endeavor to cross the continent, the Corps of Discovery—the expedition led by Meriwether Lewis and William Clark—used the path of least resistance across the wilderness of the Great Plains: the Missouri River. They embarked from St. Louis in May of 1804 with nearly fifty men, carrying supplies in a ten-ton keelboat that they had to push, pull, drag, pole, and coax upstream.

By the time they reached the upper branches of the Missouri in the mountains of Montana, they had to move their supply vessel around falls and rapids by dragging it across rolling logs for eighteen miles through rock outcroppings, cactus, bears, mosquitos, and hailstorms.

Believing they had seen the worst of it, Lewis climbed the continental divide at Lemhi Pass with hope that he would see open terrain leading to the Pacific Ocean. Imagine his reaction when he summited to see nothing but an unbroken procession of the snow-capped Rocky Mountains to the west.

The journey from St. Louis to the Oregon coast today is measured in hours, not months. While we've made straight a way through the wilderness of the American West, we still have to prepare the way of the Lord within our own hearts this Advent. Now is the time to establish a route, to smooth a path, to let go of emotional and spiritual dead weight. Reliable guides can help us navigate the terrain of this inner landscape,

14

and we will need each other on this expedition—companions to share the burdens and beauty. God's love for us is wider than a continent—there is much to discover.

Prayer for Morning

Lord, my heart has grown tangled and confused. In this wilderness, help me to make straight your path—to establish a reliable way to you. Guide my journey and give me strength to press through to you.

Spirit of wisdom, keep my feet on your path today.

Traveling Question

In what ways has my heart grown into a wilderness?

Prayer for Evening

Lord, you want to clear a pathway through the desires and distractions that tangle my heart. Help me hear your voice crying out to me, for it is the only one by which I can navigate this journey to you. Even here, at the day's end, it is not too late to hear you calling.

Spirit of wisdom, give me clarity and urgency to respond to you.

December 11

MONDAY OF THE SECOND WEEK OF ADVENT

I am sending my angel before me to prepare
the way for my coming.

The Christmas stories we know are full of angels who deliver messages in a dramatic fashion. Their appearance demonstrates God's intent to communicate with us and lead us. God continues to speak to us to direct our lives if we can listen and trust as Mary and Joseph did. Advent is the time to attune our hearts to the messages—and messengers—God sends our way.

Prayer for Morning

Heavenly Father, you sent angels to prepare a way for the birth of Jesus. You are intimately involved in my story as well, always working to draw me to yourself through the circumstances of my life. Help me recognize the heralds you send to me today.

Lord of history, give me confidence that nothing in my life is too small or insignificant to communicate your love for me.

Traveling Question

How is God speaking to me today?

Prayer for Evening

Archangels Michael, Gabriel, and Raphael, you acted as messengers for God to prepare all creation for the birth of Jesus. As I look back upon my day, help me see the situations where God was acting to prepare room in my heart for his Son, and be with me as I dwell there with him.

Archangels of God, keep me safe in God's love this night.

December 12

TUESDAY OF THE SECOND WEEK OF ADVENT

FEAST OF OUR LADY OF GUADALUPE

A great sign appeared in the sky,
a woman clothed with the sun,
with the moon under her feet,
and on her head a crown of twelve stars.

REVELATION 12:1

Next time you see an image of Our Lady of Guadalupe, pay close attention to the stars on her mantle (her cloak). Astronomers discovered that the forty-six stars arrayed around her mantle are configured in the exact arrangement of the constellations that appeared in the night sky when Mary visited St. Juan Diego for the fourth and final time on the Hill of Tepeyac outside of Mexico City on December 12, 1531.

The image that Our Lady left on Juan Diego's tilma (cape) used imagery from this verse in the book of Revelation: she stands on a crescent moon, sun rays beam all around her, and she is crowned with the stars of her mantle. The dream-like vision from Revelation describes an otherworldly figure playing a decisive role in the drama of salvation, and Mary's appearance confirms that she is this sign.

Yet, despite the cosmological scope of this appearance, Mary comes to Juan Diego—she goes so far as to seek him out—and takes on his indigenous appearance and language. She could have appeared to him in any form she liked, but she took on elements of his own culture and tenderly asked, "Am I not here, who am your mother?"

The powerful woman from Revelation—Our Lady of Guadalupe, who is arrayed with the heavens—seeks each one of us out as well. Like Juan Diego, our instinct is to recoil and to think that we are not worthy—to assume that there are too many other important people and issues for someone like Our Lady to be concerned with. Despite our objections and our uncertainty, she is our mother and will not relent until we are one with her son.

Prayer for Morning

Hail Mary, full of grace, you come to me with your motherly love and invite me to become part of the story of salvation as a protagonist—an essential participant—not a bystander. Pray that I may have the confidence and trust to respond.

Our Lady of Guadalupe, help me to become a sign, like you, of the work God is doing in the world.

Traveling Question

Who might address me today with a sign of God's love—and whom do I too easily dismiss as being capable of this kind of sign?

Prayer for Evening

Holy Mary, Mother of God, you sought out Juan Diego and equipped him to be your messenger. You have the same concern for each of us as our mother in faith. Help me carry your message of God's loving concern for each one of us.

Our Lady of Guadalupe, pray for me, that I may receive what I need to be faithful.

December 13

WEDNESDAY OF THE SECOND WEEK OF ADVENT

Be patient. Make your hearts firm,
because the coming of the Lord is at hand.
JAMES 5:7–11

Gardening is increasingly a countercultural activity because it demands so much patience. We can usually walk into a grocery store anytime and find any kind of food we want, in or out of season, but farmers know how to wait for growth, trusting in the rain and sun and earth.

Advent calls us to cultivate this kind of patience because our hearts are not steady. They wander and are tossed around by the winds of shallow desires and selfish impulses. This is a season in which to cultivate the life of grace growing within us, to extend deeper roots.

What would it take to steady our hearts, to make them firm and patient?

Prayer for Morning

Eternal Father, you are ever patient with me, even when I turn away from you. Help me to plant myself deeply in your love. Let me share your quiet patience here in the silent space of a few deep breaths.

God of growth, I am learning to trust in you.

Traveling Question

As I progress through my day, when does my heart feel steady, and when does it feel impatient?

Prayer for Evening

Lord of space and time, you are constant in your love for me, even though my heart is easily distracted. Yet you are near, even now, even here. Help me to trust that you know what I need to grow so that I am ready to welcome Christ wherever I meet him.

God of growth, grant me the patience of a steady heart.

December 14

THURSDAY OF THE SECOND WEEK OF ADVENT

Lord, our sins bring us unhappiness.
Hear our prayer for courage and strength.

We cannot prepare a way for the Lord without taking an honest look at where we have compromised God's image in ourselves and others. We think our selfishness will secure our happiness, but it always leaves us empty and unfulfilled. Worse, it leaves us feeling as if we are not worthy of God's care and concern for us, which is a lie.

Prayer for Morning

Lord God, your truth shines in my life to illuminate the shadows. You always call me toward your light. Give me strength and courage today to resist what dims your image in myself and others.

God of love, keep me close to you today.

Traveling Question

When do I feel distant from God today?

Prayer for Evening

Lord God, you created me with a deep desire for communion with you. I mistakenly fill that longing with things that are not you, with things that do not satisfy. Help me orient my heart to your loving presence, for you are the only one who can bring me to completion.

God of love, thank you for holding me close today, whether or not I was aware of your longing for me.

December 15

Friday of the Second Week of Advent

Wait for the revelation of our Lord Jesus Christ.
He will keep you firm to the end. . . . God is faithful.
1 CORINTHIANS 1:7–9

There is so much to do before Christmas, and the days are already slipping away. We know we need to fit in some Advent preparation, but it's one more thing on a to-do list that keeps growing on a calendar that keeps shrinking.

But the essence of Advent is not *doing* anything. It is, as St. Paul writes, *waiting*. God is faithful and will sustain us. Our watchfulness will reveal to us the ways God is already with us.

Prayer for Morning

Loving God, as I move through this day, open my eyes to see your Son in the people you place in my life, for you reveal yourself to me through them—each encounter is an opportunity to listen for you speaking to me. And when I recognize your Son in that fellowship, give me the grace to respond to it with a full heart.

God of faithfulness, teach me to trust you.

Traveling Question

When do I notice God sustaining me this day?

Prayer for Evening

God of abundant love, you sent your Son among us to share our troubles and help us return to you. Prepare within me the capacity to wait for you, especially when you seem absent. I know your faithfulness does not always appear in the way I expect it to, but I also know you sustain me in love.

God of faithfulness, teach me to reach for you.

December 16

SATURDAY OF THE SECOND WEEK OF ADVENT

Let us not be discouraged by our weaknesses as
we prepare for his coming.

We are not constant in our faith. We backslide, we act as if we are on our own, we lose sight of what's really important, we sink into selfishness, and we forget that the person we snapped at is a beloved child of God, just as each one of us is. Though we strive against it, this inconstancy and forgetfulness is an inescapable part of our human condition—but it does not change God's mind about us.

The important thing is that we return to God, who is ready to receive us. We don't need to be discouraged by our weakness because that's exactly where God wants to meet us.

Prayer for Morning

God, our Father, I await the healing power of Christ your Son. You sent him to reveal that nothing can stand in the way of your love for me. Be patient and merciful to me in my weakness, and come to meet me when I turn to you.

All-powerful Father, keep me steadfast in your love.

Traveling Question

When do I experience discouragement, and how can I turn that over to God today?

Prayer for Evening

God, our Father, you know my weaknesses. You also know that I am reaching for you in this Advent season, however imperfectly. Give me confidence that you are reaching for me, too, in the person of your Son, who walks with me, especially when I am weak.

All-powerful Father, help me turn to you, the source of healing.

December 17

THIRD SUNDAY OF ADVENT

Rejoice in the Lord always! I say it again. Rejoice!
Your kindness should be known to all.
The Lord is near. Have no anxiety at all,
but in everything, by prayer and petition, with thanksgiving,
Make your requests known to God.

PHILIPPIANS 4:4–7

"A heart filled with joy is more easily made perfect than one that is sad," said Philip Neri, the sixteenth-century saint who re-evangelized Rome. He's the patron saint of being cheerful—he knew laughter was attractive because it reflected joy. He collected jokes and pulled pranks and delighted in playfulness. Laughter kept him from taking himself too seriously.

Given his lightheartedness, it's ironic that he loved to pray in the dark catacombs, surrounded by the bones of Christians who had died centuries earlier. As he was praying there on the eve of Pentecost in 1544, he had a strange vision that marked the rest of his life: a globe of fire mysteriously approached him and went into his mouth. It seemed to expand inside his chest, and he was filled with euphoric rejoicing. "Enough, enough, Lord!" he exclaimed, rolling on the ground with tears of joy. "I can bear no more!"

A large bump swelled on his chest the size of his fist and remained there for the rest of his life. Though it was painless, whenever he had a spiritual insight or movement, his body could hardly contain the palpitation of his heart. At times, the lump would burn within him and he would remove his shirt to cool his chest. He was afraid he might die of

God's love. An autopsy after his death revealed that two of his ribs had broken and grown around his enlarged heart.

"Cheerfulness strengthens the heart and helps us to persevere," wrote this man who knew something about having a strong heart. "A servant of God ought always to be in good spirits."

The Lord is indeed near—nearer than we can imagine. What do we have to fear? This closeness is a cause for joy that overflows in us to lift the spirits of others.

Prayer for Morning

Lord Jesus, as I prepare to celebrate your coming at Christmas, let me even more deeply celebrate the ways you walk with me every day. Send your Spirit to help me rejoice in your love for me—and share that love with others today.

Spirit of joy, enlarge my heart with your love.

Traveling Question

When might I have an opportunity to brighten someone's day today?

Prayer for Evening

St. Philip Neri, your life—even your very body—was marked by joy. Pray for me that I can trust in God the same way you did, and that this deep confidence can move me to generosity as a way to celebrate what God has done for us.

Spirit of joy, send the fire of your love.

✦

December 18

MONDAY OF THE THIRD WEEK OF ADVENT

Tomorrow will be the day of your salvation,
the sinfulness of earth will be destroyed.
The Savior of the world will be our king.

Though Jesus was born more than two thousand years ago, sinfulness still endures, of course. The wars and injustice and oppression in force today will not disappear tomorrow. Even in our own lives, the coming Christmas feast won't make us into saints overnight. So what will change with our celebration of the arrival of this infant Son of God?

Though we still suffer from sinfulness great and small, the Lord has prevailed by preventing our sinfulness from keeping us from him. He refuses to abandon us to ourselves. He has reached for us and grasped us. In his Son, we become his children, and that changes the foundation of our identity.

Prayer for Morning

God of love, your Son was born on the day of our salvation—by becoming one of us, he changed who we are. The dignity this adoption bestows upon me is beyond anything I can earn for myself. Help me not to abuse this gift—but rather to use it to know, love, and serve you.

Jesus my King, destroy my small-minded selfishness and draw me toward your kingdom today.

Traveling Question

From what do I need saving this day?

Prayer for Evening

You have saved the world, Lord Jesus. Whether or not I acknowledge it, you have destroyed everything that can hold me back from union with our Father. I may go through life as though I am self-sufficient, but I need you to sustain me and lift me up. Life with you exceeds the goodness I can imagine for myself.

Jesus my King, save me from myself and make me yours.

✦

December 19

TUESDAY OF THE THIRD WEEK OF ADVENT

May "the dawn of his coming . . .
find us rejoicing in his presence
and welcoming the light of his truth."

This is why we have been preparing for three weeks: so that we can welcome the Lord with joy and gratitude when he comes to us. If we avoid the light of his truth because we are ashamed of what it will reveal or afraid of where it will lead us, then we live in shadows. To attune ourselves to the ways the Lord comes to us and fully rejoice when we find him, we must grow in love, for that is who God is.

Prayer for Morning

Lord Jesus, your birth was like dawn breaking upon humanity, shedding light, and bringing warmth. You make life possible for me. Though I could choose to live in shadows, I long for the freedom and fullness of your light. Help me welcome your truth today with rejoicing—not fear or shame—because I am your beloved.

Christ, our Savior, give me strength to grow in your love.

Traveling Question

What parts of my life am I content to leave in shadow?

Prayer for Evening

Lord Jesus, you are Love incarnate—the full expression of the Father's desire for union with each one of us. I celebrate your birth in Bethlehem, and I know you continue to reveal God's love to each one of us in the here and now. Be with me in this brief moment of prayer as I close this day.

Christ, our Savior, increase my longing for you.

✦

December 20

WEDNESDAY OF THE THIRD WEEK OF ADVENT

Come break down the prison walls of death for
those who dwell in darkness
and the shadow of death, and lead your captive
people into freedom.

Prisons are supposed to be secure places. Everything is controlled and locked away and watched over—nothing happens in a prison that isn't expected and planned for. And yet, they are cold, dark, spiritless places.

In small ways every day, we build for ourselves a prison of self-centeredness. Although we imagine we are somehow safer in this cell, it is lifeless there. Jesus comes to break through our prison walls, and he brings with him light, freedom, and enduring hope.

Prayer for Morning

Jesus our Savior, you come to tear down the walls that keep me stuck in complacency and self-centeredness. You are not content for me to safely seal myself away, so you arrive here in my prayer to break through the bricks I've placed around myself. May I welcome you with joy.

Lord of life, find me and lead me into your light.

Traveling Question

With what do I build my prison walls—to what am I held captive?

Prayer for Evening

Jesus broke into this world to free us from death, and he breaks into our hearts to do the same. To find freedom, I don't need to go far—I simply need to welcome this in-breaking and allow him to transform my prison into a garden. I hear you knocking, Jesus—break through these walls with your transforming love.

Lord of life, find me and lead me into freedom.

December 21

THURSDAY OF THE THIRD WEEK OF ADVENT

Let the mountains break out with joy and the hills with
answering gladness,
for the world's true light,
the Lord, comes with power and might.

It's hard to imagine mountains and hills as being joyful and glad because they are so solid and permanent. How would we know if they are laughing with one another? But that's just what this prayer invites them to do!

The boldness of this invitation is matched only by the earthshaking claim that the One who created them comes to each of us, and what's more, arrives in the most vulnerable way possible—in the person of a homeless infant. This kind of power and might is indeed a source of true joy and gladness, for it means God is with us, particularly in our fragility and brokenness and powerlessness. If we adjust our eyes, God's true light will reveal strength in weakness, solidarity in suffering, and life in death.

Prayer for Morning

Lord of earth and sky, you shape the mountains and make them joyful and glad—I know you can transform my heart, too. Your power and might become most evident when I'm willing to become small and vulnerable within your love. Make me joyful and glad as well.

God of creation, help me find you in my vulnerability.

Traveling Question

How can I make myself smaller today?

Prayer for Evening

O God, your presence reaches beneath the mountains and above the skies, yet you are most powerfully present among us in our tenderness and concern for one another. I can see that I am open to you to the degree that I am open to those in need. Help me to bring them the joy I feel in your presence.

God of creation, you reveal yourself to me in communion.

December 22

Enkindle in our hearts the flame of your love
—and make us long to be united with you.

The key to Advent is redirecting our desire. We settle far too often for shallow substitutes. Our restlessness and longing are gifts from God that pull us toward him, the only place where we will be satisfied. Advent is an opportunity to sink our hearts into that deeper longing beneath our shallow ones.

The good news is that God's love does not stay distant from us, waiting for us to make our way there. God steps toward us—*runs to us*—in his Son, Jesus. Listen! He arrives even in this moment of quiet as we start the day.

Prayer for Morning

May my prayer create an interior room where we can meet this morning, Jesus. As I try to set my heart on your love, let me do so remembering your longing for me. Help me let go of what stands between us and to embrace you fully.

Jesus, Love of the Father, kindle in me the fire of your love today.

Traveling Question

What desires are distracting me from God today?

Prayer for Evening

Because it comes from you, Jesus, the desire to embrace you is itself a way to embrace you. Help me remember that I don't have to do anything to reach you besides welcome you, who are already here with me, sparking the very longing with which I am burning.

Jesus, Love of the Father, let me rest in your love this evening.

December 23

SATURDAY OF THE THIRD WEEK OF ADVENT

Say to the fearful of heart: Be strong! Here is your God,
He comes to save you.

ISAIAH 35:4

It's easy to get stuck in small thinking. Maybe we fall back into old ways and begin to fear insignificance and lack of purpose.

But there is good news: the Lord our God is coming to save us! The Creator of time and space—the one who made the land and the sea—is wholly concerned with each one of us. We have already felt him near.

As Psalm 124 reminds us, "Our help is in the name of the Lord, who made heaven and earth." What do we have to fear?

Prayer for Morning

Almighty God, you sent your Son, Jesus, to save us from death. You continue to send him into my life to give me life. When I am in need—even with the smallest of problems—may I turn to him today with trust in your saving power.

Jesus our Savior, give me courage to rely on you today.

Traveling Question

Whom will I meet in need of courage today?

Prayer for Evening

Almighty God, you are with me wherever I go. You know what drains my confidence, where I lack strength, and how my heart is inconstant. Strengthen my faith so I can trust in your ever-present care for me and revel in the gratuitous gift that it is.

Spirit of hope, with gratitude I rest in your providing love.

December 24

FOURTH SUNDAY OF ADVENT
AND CHRISTMAS EVE

Father in heaven, the day draws near
when the glory of your Son
will make radiant the night of the waiting world.
May the darkness not blind us to the vision of wisdom
which fills the minds of those who find him.

The ancient Greeks associated owls with wisdom because they observed these birds navigating darkness so precisely. It was thought that these predators had an inner light or mystical vision by which to see. Owls do have excellent night vision with their unusually large eyes, but they also have extraordinary hearing.

The feathers of their round faces function like a satellite dish, funneling sound to their ears. And one ear is slightly closer to their face than the other, which allows them to triangulate sound. It's stunning evolutionary technology that allows owls to hear mice in the dark, even 100 yards away, *even under a foot of snow*.

Darkness does not blind owls because they have sharpened their senses to perceive what is not visible. That's why they appear wise—they don't depend solely on what they can see. They are highly attuned to the invisible world.

This is a good description of the relationship between wisdom and faithfulness. Wisdom helps us look beneath the surface to understand what is important and essential even when it is hidden. A life of faith means being attuned to invisible realities like faith, hope, and love—especially when they are not evident.

Throughout this Advent journey, we have been sharpening our senses to perceive God coming to us in his Son. Finding him deepens our wisdom, our ability to see in the darkness.

After developing our ability to wait with patience these last weeks, we will celebrate Christ's birth tomorrow, which heightens the hopeful expectation that he will come into each of our lives anew—and will come again at the end of time—to make radiant our night.

Prayer for Morning

Lord of light, you come to me each day and suffuse my life with faith, hope, and love. Help me not to be fooled or distracted today—help me to see you, especially when my vision gets narrowed by all the noise and motion around me, and to hold onto you here with me.

Jesus, Light of the World, sharpen my senses that I may find you today.

Traveling Question

What dulls my senses at this busy time, blocking my perception of God's presence with me and within me?

Prayer for Evening

Lord of light, you illuminate that which gives my life meaning. As night descends, I continue to look for your light. In my search for you, I am finding that you've been searching for me all along. In my waiting for you, I discover you waiting for me. You are always a step closer than I imagine. I reach for you and am already in your grasp.

Jesus, Light of the World, come with your radiant love.

December 25

The Nativity of the Lord

Almighty God and Father of light, . . .
your eternal Word leaped down from heaven in the
silent watches of the night,
and now your Church is filled with wonder
at the nearness of her God.

In his Incarnation, Jesus didn't merely descend to us from heaven—he *leaped*.

If you know someone who has ever gone skydiving, ask them about it. The most vivid part of their story will be the moment they jumped from the plane, guaranteed. They'll tell you what it felt like to be in an aircraft skittering up into the sky, aluminum rattling beneath their feet. They'll tell you about the moment they dreaded the most: when the door opened—the buzz of the engine rushing in like angry bees and the cold air swirling in like a small tornado.

When it was their time, they had to move to the opening and push their feet over the edge, the wind battering their shoes. And there came a moment when all the preparation and anticipation had reached an end—a decisive moment when they either leaped into the wild air or drew back into the safety of the plane.

When they made the decision to leap, they were irrevocably committed. Once they were past the edge of the door and falling, there was no way to change course and climb back into the plane.

Jesus leaped into our humanity with the same commitment. In sending him, our Father revealed he is permanently *with us*—he has chosen us irreversibly. And what's true for all of us is true for each one of us—Jesus leaps into our individual lives, too. He leaps into our

Christmas parties, our to-do lists, our anxiety, our unsettled relationships, our diet plan, our career aspirations, our waiting at the post office, our vacation plans, our illnesses, our loneliness, our calls back home, our joy, and our sorrow.

He wants to be with us in everything—he's all in. Are we?

Prayer for Morning

Lord Jesus Christ, you are God's Word to us, the definitive communication of the Father's love for each one of us. May I tune the ear of my heart to hear and receive you, and wonder at the gift of this love.

Jesus, Word of the Father, help me hear you speaking in my life today.

Traveling Question

Because of God's commitment to me, nothing in my life is too small to elicit wonder—where will I find it today?

Prayer for Evening

Lord Jesus Christ, you came to show us how near God is. Beneath the gifts and lights and music and sweets, at the wonder-filled core of this Christmas feast is the radical belief that in you, God reaches out to share life with me. Be near to me now, at the end of this day of celebration.

Jesus, Word of the Father, enflame my heart with your nearness.

December 26

TUESDAY IN THE OCTAVE OF CHRISTMAS

By the mystery of your incarnation
we are made your brothers and sisters.

With the birth of his Son, God became part of our human family. What a remarkable gift: our Creator descended to become part of creation. By so completely joining our human family—by sharing our human condition, even our death—Jesus has changed our destiny. As C. S. Lewis wrote, "The Son of God became man to enable men to become the sons of God." We are children of God—his sons and daughters—because God became a child.

Prayer for Morning

Jesus, you made us your siblings and join us on our way to our Father in heaven. We wonder at the gift of becoming part of God's family! Walk with me today so I may recognize how I was thought of and chosen from eternity—that I am precious in our Father's eyes.

Jesus my brother, lift me up to the Father today.

Traveling Question

What threatens my dignity as God's child? What threatens the dignity of people in my community?

Prayer for Evening

Jesus, your birth changed everything about the human condition. You changed everything about my identity by allowing me to become God's own child. Give me faithfulness to match this gift so I may never become estranged from God's family.

Jesus my brother, keep me close to you.

December 27

WEDNESDAY IN THE OCTAVE OF CHRISTMAS

> Lord, fill your holy people with whatever good they need
> —let the mystery of your birth be the source of our peace.

We search for peace—for rest, fulfillment, and satisfaction—in many places. We reach for objects and experiences to quiet our restlessness. Though we fill our lives with good things, they always pass away, and we become hungry again.

There is only one source of lasting peace. What is more, we don't need to reach for anything because he reaches for us. If we open our lives to be held by him, we will be at rest.

Prayer for Morning

Almighty God, you are all good, and your creation reflects your goodness and speaks of you. Help me find you with wonder in the good things around me, and then turn to you in my need today. You walk with me and will sustain me with the gift of life you share through your Son.

Lord Jesus, Prince of Peace, fill me with whatever good I need today.

Traveling Question

What are the lesser goods I sometimes reach for in my search for peace?

Prayer for Evening

Almighty God, you know what I need and supply it in your will to draw me to you. Help me rest in the faith that you are here with me now, and that the free gift of your love for me does not depend on my worthiness of it.

Spirit of peace, I offer you my wonder and gratitude.

December 28

Thursday in the Octave of Christmas

The holy Virgin gave birth to God
who became for us the frail, tender baby she
nursed at her breast.
Let us worship the Lord who comes to save us.

This newborn is the Lord who comes to save us? This infant who cannot control his own body is the one who rules over the movement of the stars? This baby who is utterly dependent on his parents for survival is the one who brings us life?

This is the mystery we celebrate with wonder in our Christmas feast: that God comes to us by becoming small and vulnerable. When we imitate that humility, we will discover the secret place where we can meet this child.

Prayer for Morning

Lord Jesus, you embraced frailness and dependency to join us in our humanity. Help me embrace the same humility when I am confronted with challenges that threaten my autonomy and sting my pride today. I know you are with me when I am feeling small.

Jesus our Savior, help me find you in moments of tenderness today.

Traveling Question

When will I have the opportunity to practice humility today?

Prayer for Evening

Mother Mary, your humility opened a way for God to visit us in your child, Jesus. Here at the end of my day, help me review the ways God visited me today, especially when I was too full of myself to pay attention.

Mary, our mother, draw me into the intimacy you share with Jesus.

December 29

Friday in the Octave of Christmas

God of love, Father of all, . . . make us faithful to your Word,
that we may bring your life to the waiting world.

God could save the world in any manner he chose, so what does it say
that he saved us by becoming one of us and leading us toward himself?
It means he wants our participation in our own salvation.

Faith is a gift that we welcome and cultivate. When we receive God's
Word and let him change us, we find that we have good news to proclaim and join Jesus's mission to bring life to a world waiting for light.

Prayer for Morning

God our Father, encountering your love is transformative; the wonder and gratitude we share for the gift of your Son moves us outward.
Help me notice others in my life today who need a sign of your love
for them, too.

Spirit of life, make me attentive to your promptings today.

Traveling Question

Who is waiting for good news, and how can I speak God's Word to
them today?

Prayer for Evening

God, our Father, Mary was faithful to your Word and bore your Son to
our waiting world. Help me imitate her openness and trust, and dispel
any fear I have of where you might lead me. Wherever it is, I know you
will lead me into life.

Mother Mary, help me place my life in God's hands as you did.

December 30

Saturday in the Octave of Christmas

Christ, born of the Father before the ages,
splendor of his glory,
image of his being, your word holds all creation in being.

At some point today, you will interact with the created world. You'll wash a tomato before dinner and notice the water beading on its skin. Or you'll step outside and draw clean, fresh air in through your nose. Or you'll feel the sun warming your back as it streams in a window behind you.

None of these things needed to be, but they are—and their goodness raises our eyes to our Creator. God did not create the world to set it free to wander into death. God created the world and then joined it, himself, in order to save it. The best way to respond to this gift is with the simple acknowledgment of wonder and gratitude.

Prayer for Morning

God of creation, you do not remain at a distance but come to dwell with us through our relationship with your Son, Jesus. The goodness I experience in your created world draws me to you and reminds me that I am part of your creation, myself—that my very life is a gift. Help me to dwell with you today.

Jesus, Word of the Father, help me see and hear you today.

Traveling Question

When will I have the chance to offer gratitude today?

Prayer for Evening

God of creation, you breathed on the emerging world and made it good. You continue to breathe your life in me, which sustains me—in fact, you are closer to me than is my own breathing. In your Son, you have joined my life, and through him, you will raise me to live with you.

Jesus, Word of the Father, thank you for holding me near you today.

December 31

Sunday in the Octave of Christmas

And Feast of the Holy Family

Father, help us to live as the holy family,
united in respect and love.
Bring us to the joy and peace of your eternal home.

Family isn't easy. Every family has its own frictions, and the Holy Family was no different. What made Jesus, Mary, and Joseph holy as a family was not that they got along well all the time. Being holy is not the same thing as being nice.

In fact, we can assume that there was a lot of tension in that family at times. Imagine the looks Mary and Joseph shared when they met up after a full day of travel to realize they'd left Jesus behind in one of the biggest cities in the world. Or their discussions about leaving everything behind—home, livelihood, and family—and fleeing to Egypt, where they didn't know the people or customs. Tradition holds that Joseph died before the start of Jesus's public ministry because he is absent from those accounts, so we can also assume that this was a family that dealt with profound grief.

What made the Holy Family holy is articulated in today's prayer: they were united in respect and love. Regardless of how functional a family is or isn't, everyone can offer those two things. We can respect that every family member is a beloved child of God with their own unique journey of faithfulness, just as we are beloved and unique. And we can love every family member by willing their greatest good.

With respect and love, we strive for unity, which will be fully realized one day when we find each other in union with God.

Prayer for Morning

Spirit of love, you guided the Holy Family as they navigated their central role in salvation history, giving them what they needed to fulfill everything that was asked of them. Give me what I need to navigate life with my family and help us move toward unity in our joys and challenges.

Holy Spirit, help my family grow in faith, hope, and love today.

Traveling Question

What opportunity will I find today to show respect and love for my family?

Prayer for Evening

Jesus, Mary, and Joseph, your love for one another gave you strength and courage to follow where God our Father was leading, even when it was difficult or confusing. Strengthen and encourage my family that we may be a sign to others of the joy and peace that God intends for us.

Holy Family, grant us your peace this evening.

January 1

MONDAY IN THE OCTAVE OF CHRISTMAS

SOLEMNITY OF MARY, MOTHER OF GOD

And Mary kept all these things,
reflecting on them in her heart.

LUKE 2:19

The shepherds arriving after Jesus's birth must have been a surprise. Mary and Joseph knew there was something special about the child, and Mary's cousin, Elizabeth, had said the same. But now, for the first time, this little life was touching complete strangers.

And they must have looked strange—and smelled even stranger. These were outsiders, and they arrived with wide eyes and fantastical stories about the heavens opening up and a message from an angel. How did they know what was going on with this little family so far from home?

When the shepherds left, they continued to share the news about shining angels coming in the night with tidings of joy and praise. According to Luke, everyone who heard their tale was amazed, which is easy to imagine. It's quite a story, and the fact that it came from shepherds probably made it good grist for the gossip mill. But Mary knew differently—she "kept these things, reflecting on them in her heart."

That one small line tells us quite a bit about Mary. She had just carried and delivered to us God's Son. Though that was a task that bent history, she didn't stop pondering, searching, thinking, hoping, and waiting for God to speak to her. She continued to read her experience through the lens of her faith—it was a way of life for her. It was wonderous, and likely terrifying, when God sent an angel to speak to her, but she also knew how to listen for God's voice in the ordinary experiences of her life.

Prayer for Morning

Hail Mary, full of grace, you were committed to prayer and reflection—a journey I am walking as well. I am not perfect, but I trust you to help me to be faithful to these habits, so that I may become more alive in God's Spirit, and bear God's Word to the world as you did.

Mary, our mother, help me listen for God's Word speaking within me today.

Traveling Question

When will I find a moment to reflect in my heart this day?

Prayer for Evening

Holy Mary, Mother of God, your life of faithfulness led you to many surprises. Through it all, you trusted in God. I don't know what tomorrow will hold, but I know that God holds me with the same tenderness he held you. That closeness is enough for now—God will lead me through whatever is ahead.

Mary, our mother, help me rest in the love of your Son this night.

January 2

*May the simple beauty of Jesus' birth summon us always
to love what is most deeply human,
and to see your Word made flesh reflected in those whose
lives we touch.*

Because God shares our humanity in Jesus Christ, we do not need to search for God in some distant place. The search for God's presence moves us inward and deeper into our own stories. Our memories and experiences and longings are all places where God speaks to us. Being in a beautiful cathedral lifts our spirits, but God is just as content to meet us when we turn to him in the stillness of our hearts.

This journey inward and deeper is not self-involved, however—it spins us outward. The more we encounter and are changed by God's self-giving love, the more we are drawn to imitate it by offering ourselves to others.

Prayer for Morning

Lord Jesus, you raised our dignity by joining our humanity. My adoption into God's family joins me inseparably to others in that family that shares my dignity. Raise my awareness of how I can better love my neighbor.

Loving Father, help me reflect your self-giving love today.

Traveling Question

Who will touch my life today in a way that reveals your Word to me?

Prayer for Evening

Lord Jesus, God's Word made flesh, you did not hold back anything from us, even when our humanity showed you our worst—when we betrayed and mocked and killed you. Your love conquers all, even the worst parts of us. Help me believe that nothing can stand in the way of your love for me.

Loving Father, let me rest in your unconditional love this night.

January 3

WEDNESDAY IN THE CHRISTMAS SEASON

Concerning the Word of life. . .
What we have seen and heard we proclaim to you now so that
you, too, may have fellowship with us;
for our fellowship is with the Father
and with his Son, Jesus Christ.

1 JOHN 1:1, 3

Our spiritual journey through the Advent and Christmas seasons is meant to deepen our connection to others who walk with us, and to strengthen our bonds to those who have walked before us in faith and those who will walk after us.

John wrote his letter that is quoted above from within a specific community trying to make sense of life in the light of Jesus's birth, life, death, and resurrection. As a Christian community, we've held on to his words for a reason—we pass them on because they draw us into the same search for meaning, and point to an answer: we are part of a communion of faithful people who through the ages have followed the way of Jesus.

Prayer for Morning

Spirit of life, you guide our community of faith through the centuries, helping us walk in the way of Jesus. Help me follow his way so that my life reflects your divine life more clearly. Increase my faith, hope, and love so that what people see and hear from me proclaims the Word of Life.

Jesus, Word of Life, speak through me today.

Traveling Question

Where will I hear words of life today?

Prayer for Evening

Spirit of life, you put us in communion with all of the faithful who have gone before us—you offer us their friendship as an aid in our journey. May their faith give me confidence to trust God with my life, knowing that he will keep me safe in his love, no matter what my future holds.

Jesus, Word of Life, I trust in you.

January 4

THURSDAY IN THE CHRISTMAS SEASON

He comes in splendor, the King who is our peace;
the whole world longs to see him.

What a strange thing to say—that Jesus comes in splendor! We know the story: he came as a helpless infant, arriving without a home or a bed and two travel-weary newlyweds for parents, and they had to flee for his life almost immediately. Would it not be more accurate to say that he came in *powerlessness*?

Yet this is the whole point of his birth: he opened a way for God to meet us in our vulnerability. By entering our most broken places, God forever joined the human and the divine. The child Jesus became the meeting place between heaven and earth.

Prayer for Morning

Prince of Peace, you are with us in all things, and have the power to use our powerlessness as a means for our good. Give me the faith to be able to see glory in vulnerability, not to fear it, for it leads me to depend upon you alone.

Jesus, our King, meet me in vulnerability today.

Traveling Question

What will I do when I encounter powerlessness this day?

Prayer for Evening

Prince of Peace, the whole world longs for the rest only you can offer. I come to you with the burdens I carry and offer them to you, knowing nothing is too small or minor for your help. I don't expect you to take them away from me, but your companionship and strength will help me carry them.

Jesus, our King, be my source of peace.

January 5

FRIDAY IN THE CHRISTMAS SEASON

Give thanks to the Father, who has made you fit
to share the inheritance of the holy ones in light.

COLOSSIANS 1:12

In Jesus, God has made us worthy of the same light that shines from the saints and angels. In him, we are partakers in divine life, destined for communion with God forever.

We didn't do anything to become worthy of this gift—there's nothing we *could* do to become worthy of it. It is freely offered because this is who God is: self-gift. God could no more withhold this love than a tree could withhold shade. Our part is simple—to give thanks.

Prayer for Morning

Merciful Father, you created us for eternity with you. This destiny is too high, too wide, and too far for us to imagine, so you came to us in your Son to walk with us there through whatever trials we face. Expand my hope so I keep the light of this vision before me.

Father, keep my heart set on you today.

Traveling Question

How might I offer thanks to God today?

Prayer for Evening

Merciful Father, your saints live with you in the light of everlasting love. As darkness falls on the earth this evening, continue to shine in my life. I come before you with the only thing I can offer in return for the gift of your love: my gratitude and wonder.

Father, I give you thanks for the way you illuminate my life.

January 6

SATURDAY IN THE CHRISTMAS SEASON

While earth was rapt in silence and night only
half through its course,
your mighty Word, O Lord, came down from
his royal throne, alleluia.

Although too early to detect, light is returning to our days now that the sun is beginning its march toward summer. Every day we gain back minutes of light, reminding us of the hope that has dawned in our world with the coming of Jesus. From the moment of his birth, light has shone in our darkness.

Though Jesus is God's Word, he came to us in silence. He arrived in a hidden, quiet way—and he continues to come to us in stillness. Silence is a privileged way for us to hear God speaking; when we cultivate stillness in our hearts, we make room for the Word.

Prayer for Morning

Lord Jesus, Light of the World, the darkness of uncertainty and emptiness is not foreign to you. When I feel alone and lost, send your Spirit to illuminate my way. Help me to find you here with me.

Word of God, help me hear you speaking to me today.

Traveling Question

How will I make room for silence today?

Prayer for Evening

Spirit of light and truth, you draw us to communion with the Father through Jesus our brother. The dawn of his coming broke into our world in a quiet and hidden way. Be with me here in the silence of this evening, that his light might shine and burn within me.

Word of God, meet me in this stillness.

January 7

EPIPHANY SUNDAY

May he be like rain coming down upon the fields,
like showers watering the earth,
That abundance may flourish in his days,
great bounty, till the moon be no more.

PSALM 72:6–7

There's a word for that wet, earthy scent that emerges just as rain begins to fall: *petrichor*. The smell comes from ozone (created by lightning and carried downward by water droplets), plants releasing aromatic oils, and a molecule called *geosmin*, which is produced by bacteria in the soil.

The human nose is highly attuned to geosmin—we can detect it in levels as low as five parts per trillion. Some scientists believe that our bodies became sensitive to geosmin because our ancestors relied on rainwater for survival—the substance came to signal an important change in weather that we needed to be ready for. Even now that we have reliable sources of water, petrichor usually stops us in our tracks with a breath of wonder.

Humans are also finely attuned to hope. It's not a scent, but we do perceive it on the parts-per-trillion scale. We notice someone whose life is marked by hope because they seem to run with a different motor—they have resilience and joy; they live abundantly. We need these things to survive, too.

Something like wonder and hope drew the Magi over the desert to Bethlehem to find our newborn Savior. They were searching for a deeper order to reality—a way to make sense of the world—and sensed something new in the changes they observed in the astronomical weather. So, they packed up and followed their noses.

We are all searching for meaning, too—we are all on a journey to make sense of our place in the world. Unless you're an astronomer, your tools are different than what the Magi used, but the same desire is pulling you. It's the smell of hope.

Prayer for Morning

Lord Jesus, your birth drew visitors far and wide who were searching for the life you bring. I know the people I will meet today—even in passing—are also searching for your life. Direct my decisions and actions so that others may discern your presence as my guiding star.

Jesus, our Savior, deepen my faith, hope, and love.

Traveling Question

What am I searching for today, and what signs are speaking to me?

Prayer for Evening

Lord Jesus, the Magi who found you were searching for royalty but found a homeless infant. They were open enough to change their expectations, however, and recognized in you what they were looking for. Help me adjust my vision to see you in places I might not expect.

Jesus, our Savior, I come before you to offer the gift of my life.

January 8

FEAST OF THE BAPTISM OF THE LORD

The spirit of the Lord GOD is upon me,
because the LORD has anointed me;
He has sent me to bring good news to the afflicted,
to bind up the brokenhearted,
To proclaim liberty to the captives,
release to the prisoners,
To announce a year of favor from the LORD
and a day of vindication by our God;
To comfort all who mourn.

ISAIAH 61:1–2

Jesus's baptism marks the beginning of his public ministry—in the gospels, this event serves as the transition point between the early years of his birth and the accounts of his adult life spent teaching and healing.

In fact, in the Gospel of Luke, Jesus begins his public ministry by appearing in the synagogue in Nazareth and proclaiming these words from the prophet Isaiah. They function as a mission statement for him—he is here to fulfill the vision of a Savior who is sent to the lonely and brokenhearted. His mission is to proclaim good news to the poor and liberty to captives.

In the stillness of prayer these past weeks, we've felt God's nearness to us, especially in our darkness. This is exactly why God sent Jesus—to bring us glad tidings and heal our broken hearts.

Reflecting on Jesus's baptism also concludes our Advent journey and Christmas feasting. Today's feast calls to mind our own baptisms, which allow our lives to take the same shape as Jesus's life, death, and resurrection. Having been immersed into the life of Christ in his Church, our next step is to take up our role in its mission.

Jesus didn't come to save us as mere individuals. He came to save us as a people, to welcome us collectively to his mission of drawing into

God's kingdom all of humanity, indeed all of creation. The baptism we share with him makes us ready to get to work.

Prayer for Morning

Holy Spirit, in our baptism, you shared God's life with us. Deepen my faith that I may imitate Jesus. In following his way, may I come to embody his life and love for the world.

Spirit of the Lord, send me out with your Good News today.

Traveling Question

Who is lonely or brokenhearted in my life today? What good news can I share with them?

Prayer for Evening

Lord Jesus Christ, here at the end of this celebration of your birth, I give you thanks for the many ways you come to me. Thank you for walking with me these past weeks. Be with me in the days ahead that I may continue walking in your way.

Spirit of the Lord, deepen my faith and raise me to new life in Christ.

Founded in 1865 by Fr. Edward Sorin, CSC, **Ave Maria Press** is an apostolate of the Congregation of Holy Cross, United States Province of Priests and Brothers. Ave is a nonprofit Catholic publishing ministry that serves the spiritual and formative needs of the Church and its schools, institutions, and ministers; Christian individuals and families; and others seeking spiritual nourishment.

Ave remains one of the oldest continually operating Catholic publishing houses in the country and a leader in publishing Catholic high school religion textbooks, ministry resources, and books on prayer and spirituality.

In the tradition of Holy Cross, Ave is committed, as an educator in the faith, to help people know, love, and serve God and to spread the Gospel of Jesus Christ through books and other resources.

Ave Maria Press perpetuates Fr. Sorin's vision to honor Mary and provide an important outlet for good Catholic writing.

DON'T MISS
TURN TO THE CROSS
DAILY PRAYERS FOR LENT
AND HOLY WEEK 2024

In *Turn to the Cross*, each day from Ash Wednesday through Easter Sunday begins with a passage from the Liturgy of the Hours, followed by a short spiritual reflection, morning and evening prayers, and a question to ponder throughout the day. About five minutes a day is all we need as we turn to the Cross for healing, hope, and renewal.

EACH WEEK INCLUDES A NEW LENTEN THEME:

· God is faithful
· the call to conversion
· loving others by giving alms
· self-denial through fasting
· union with God in prayer
· following Christ through the Cross

"Deeply thought-provoking and hugely helpful in praying through the Church's high seasons."

—Katie Prejean McGrady
Host of the *Ave Explores* podcast and *The Katie McGrady Show* on Sirius XM's The Catholic Channel